HUNGRY

COOKING OUTDOORS FOR 1 TO 100

CAMPERS

WRITTEN AND PHOTOGRAPHED BY ZAC WILLIAMS

GIBBS SMITH
TO ENRICH AND INSPIRE HUMANKIND

For Jennifer, who always first inspires.

First Edition
17 16 15 14 13   5 4 3 2 1

Text and photographs © 2013 Zac Williams

Published by
Gibbs Smith
P.O. Box 667
Layton, Utah 84041

1.800.835.4993 orders
www.gibbs-smith.com

Designed by Sowins Design
Printed and bound in Hong Kong

Gibbs Smith books are printed on paper produced from sustainable PEFC-
certified forest/controlled wood source. Learn more at www.pefc.org.

Library of Congress Cataloging-in-Publication Data

Williams, Zac.
  Hungry campers : cooking outdoors for 1 to 100 / written and
photographed by Zac Williams. — First edition.
    pages cm
  ISBN 978-1-4236-3028-9
1. Outdoor cooking. I. Title.
  TX823.W523 2013
  641.5′78—dc23
                        2012033196

Contents

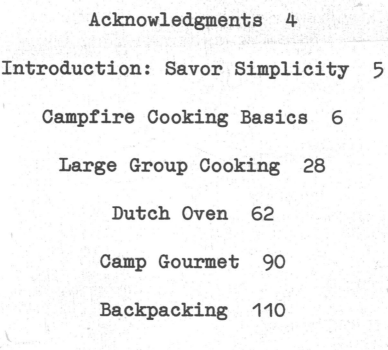

Acknowledgments

I would like to thank everyone at Gibbs Smith for the opportunity to have so much fun writing and photographing with special thanks to Hollie Keith for expert editing and Suzanne Taylor for making it all possible. Thanks to Rita Sowins for the terrific design of the book. Continued thanks to my wife, Aimee, and kids, Ethan, Rya and Piper, for putting up with a crazy cooking dad and always waiting to taste until after I get the shot.

Introduction:
Savor Simplicity

Camping is all about taking a detour from day-to-day life. Spending time sleeping outdoors tends to remind us of what's important. It takes us back to the basics of comfort. A dry bed, good company and of course delicious food are all you need to enjoy yourself in the wild. Delicious food is where this cookbook comes in. By focusing on simple, easy-to-prepare meals, I hope to help campers make the most of their time outdoors.

Recipes are arranged in chapters beginning with ideas for meals that are easy to prepare and teach basic cooking skills, and progress to more advanced gourmet preparations for those camp chefs who are looking for inspiration. Special attention is given to making the job of planning dining operations for scout troops, youth groups and families easier. Along the way, helpful tips are suggested to make your cooking experience even better. For campers and scouts looking for high adventure, an introduction to backpack cooking with recipes and menus is provided in the last chapter.

Hopefully, this cookbook can serve as a primer for new cooks as well as a resource that makes planning easier for experienced campers. Fine dining should be at the center of any great camping adventure. My favorite childhood memories of camping include watching as my dad cooked on the old green double-burner Coleman stove. Now I share my own son's excitement as he cooks the trout he just caught. Outdoor cooking properly done is one of the many joys experienced by those that trade a roof at home for the starry sky overhead.

Campfire Cooking Basics

For those new to camp cooking, a great place to start is with the basics. Cooking over a fire is perfect because all campers can participate in preparing, cooking and eating! Perfect for overnight camping trips, these basic recipes also require minimal equipment to prepare and clean up easily. Each recipe serves one.

Stadium Brats

Serves 1

1 bratwurst sausage
1/2 small onion, sliced
1 teaspoon butter

1 large roll or hot
  dog bun, slit
Deli mustard or
  other condiments

Equipment

Campfire coals
Heavy-duty
  aluminum foil

1. Place bratwurst, sliced onion and butter on a sheet of aluminum foil, shiny side facing up. Wrap securely, taking care to fold edges tightly. Place on the coals and cook 15–20 minutes, turning frequently.

2. Serve cooked sausage on the bun and smother with cooked onions. Season with deli mustard or other condiments.

Brown Bag Campfire Breakfast

Serves 1

3 strips bacon
2 eggs
¹/₂ cup frozen hash
  brown potatoes,
  thawed

Salt
Black pepper
Hot pepper sauce
  (optional)

Equipment

Campfire coals
Brown paper bag
  (lunch size)
Stick or marshmallow
  roasting fork

1. Place bacon in the bottom of the bag. Crack eggs into the bag over the bacon. Add hash brown potatoes. Season with salt and black pepper to taste.

2. Fold and roll down the top of the bag until about 3 inches above the potatoes. Insert a stick through folded portion and cook 5–6 inches over low coals for about 10 minutes. It helps to prop up the stick with rocks.

3. Carefully tear off the top of the bag to serve. Season with hot pepper sauce.

Sunnyside Sandwich

Serves 1

2 eggs
2 slices bread,
  thick Texas toast
1 slice cheddar cheese
1–2 single-serve
  mayonnaise packets
Salt
Black pepper

Equipment

2 large waxed
  paper cups filled
  with water
Barbecue tongs with
  a long handle
Heavy leather gloves

Campfire coals
Sheet of heavy-duty
  aluminum foil

1. Place each egg into one of the cups filled with water. Using the tongs and gloves, carefully place each cup on the hot coals. Allow water to boil for 6 minutes, until eggs are soft-boiled.

2. While eggs are boiling, place slices of bread on the sheet of aluminum foil, shiny side facing up, and toast at the edge of the fire for 5 minutes.

3. Carefully remove eggs from the fire with the tongs. Crack and serve between the slices of toasted bread with the cheese and mayonnaise. Season with salt and black pepper to taste.

Box Turnovers

Serves 2–4

1 can refrigerated
  biscuits
1 (10.25-ounce) jar
  jam (strawberry,
  raspberry or peach
  works well)
Decorating sugar

Equipment

Open-top cardboard box
  (copy paper size)
Heavy-duty
  aluminum foil
Campfire coals
3 rocks or bricks
  about 5 inches tall

Small baking sheet
  or pie tin
Fire-resistant
  mitt or tongs

1. Cover box completely on all sides, inside and out, with 2 layers of aluminum foil, shiny side facing out, making sure no cardboard is visible.

2. Open refrigerated biscuits, separate and flatten each one slightly. Spoon jam into the center of each round of biscuit dough. Fold over and pinch edges to seal. Sprinkle generously with decorating sugar. Place the turnovers on the baking sheet or in the pie tin.

3. Over low coals (no flames), place 3 rocks or bricks into a tripod shape to support the cookie sheet or pie tin. Lower cardboard box over turnovers and bake 8–12 minutes, checking every few minutes.

The box oven can also be used to make rolls, biscuits and mini cupcakes or to cook small pizzas.

Pizza Pitas with Garlic Bread

Serves 1

2 flatbread pita
  rounds
2 tablespoons pizza
  or marinara sauce
1/4 cup shredded
  mozzarella cheese
Assorted pizza toppings
  (pepperoni, diced
  ham, mushrooms,
  canned pineapple,
  green bell pepper
  slices, sliced
  black olives)
Italian seasoning

1 loaf French bread
1/2 cup butter
1/2-1 teaspoon garlic
  powder, or to taste

Equipment

Campfire coals
Heavy-duty
  aluminum foil

1. Place 1 pita round on a sheet of aluminum foil, shiny side facing up. Spread sauce over pita and add cheese and toppings as desired. Sprinkle with Italian seasoning to taste.

2. Cover with the remaining pita.

3. Wrap aluminum foil over pitas and fold in edges to seal. Place over coals and cook 10–12 minutes, turning once halfway through.

4. Cut French bread into slices three-quarters of the way through. Stuff each slit with butter and garlic powder. Wrap loaf in aluminum foil and cook on coals about 10–12 minutes.

Zip Bag Salad

Serves 1

2 cups iceberg
  lettuce, chopped

2 tablespoons grated
  Parmesan cheese
2 tablespoons prepared
  Italian dressing

Equipment

1 quart-size Ziploc
  freezer bag

Combine all ingredients in the Ziploc bag and shake to coat. Eat out of the bag or empty onto a plate.

★★

Classic Tinfoil Dinner

Serves 1

1¹/₃ ground beef
  patty, thawed
Ground black pepper
Garlic salt

1 cup cubed potatoes
¹/₂ cup baby carrots
¹/₂ sliced onion
2 tablespoons ketchup

Equipment

Campfire coals
Heavy-duty
  aluminum foil

1. Place the ground beef patty on a sheet of aluminum foil, shiny side facing up, and season with black pepper and garlic salt to taste. Add potatoes, carrots and onion and top with ketchup. Fold the long sides of the aluminum foil inward and seal. Roll short ends securely into the middle.

2. Place wrapped dinner on coals and cook 10 minutes on each side. Open carefully to avoid steam burns, and serve.

In place of ketchup, substitute half a can of cream of mushroom soup for a delicious variation.

Constructing a Cooking Fire

Successful campfire cooking starts before you strike a match. It is important to build a proper fire to quickly create an even bed of hot coals. A good fire requires heat, fuel and oxygen. A log cabin–style fire, where wood is successively stacked in a square much like a pioneer's log cabin, allows for plenty of air circulation as well as an even spacing of fuel. This type of fire also creates a perfect bed of coals. Wood used in a fire should be dry and preferably seasoned, meaning it comes from a dead tree or was cut months earlier. Hardwoods such as trimmings from fruit trees make better coals than softwoods such as pine and fir. When starting the fire, tinder of crumpled paper, wood shavings or other loose flammable material should be ignited under the bottom layer of the fire. Many effective commercial fire-starting products are available that allow for a hot ignition. A properly built fire won't require much tending to create a hot, even bed of coals.

Easy Lemon Butter Trout

Serves 1

1 fresh trout,
   cleaned and dressed
   (8–12 inches)
2 tablespoons
   butter, softened

1 teaspoon lemon
   pepper
Tarter sauce
   (optional)

Equipment

Heavy-duty
   aluminum foil
Campfire coals

1. Place trout on a sheet of aluminum foil, shiny side facing up. Spread butter along the inside of the fish. While holding the fish open, sprinkle lemon pepper liberally over butter. Wrap fish in foil, sealing edges and ends well. Place the wrapped fish seam side down and repeat the wrap with a second sheet of foil.

2. Place on coals for 8–12 minutes, depending on the size of the trout. When cooked, the meat will pull away from the bones, which can be easily removed and discarded. The skin will slide off. Serve with tarter sauce.

Baked Caramel Apples

Serves 1

1 golden delicious
   apple

3–4 soft caramel
   candies
1 tablespoon butter

Equipment

Campfire coals
Aluminum foil

1. Cut out the top $^3/_4$ of the core of the apple, taking care not to cut through the bottom. Place 3 or 4 caramel candies into the hollowed-out apple and top with butter.

2. Wrap apple in aluminum foil and place right side up on coals. Cook for 12–14 minutes, until apple is soft and caramel is melted. If necessary, stir butter and caramel to mix.

★★★

Banana Boats

Serves 1

1 banana
$^1/_4$ cup chocolate chips
Mini marshmallows

Equipment

Campfire coals
Heavy-duty
   aluminum foil

1. Cut banana peel into a 1-inch-wide flap down the length of the banana, leaving skin attached at the bottom. Open the flap and cut a row of notches out of the banana, leaving space between each banana square.

2. Stuff each space with chocolate chips and a mini marshmallow. Replace flap of banana and wrap in aluminum foil, shiny side facing up. Place on coals, leaving the stem side up, and cook for 8–10 minutes. Unwrap and serve.

Simple S'mores

		Equipment
1 bag large marshmallows	1 package fudge-covered graham cracker cookies	Campfire coals Cooking sticks

Roast a marshmallow on a stick over a fire, turning frequently. When hot and toasty, slide onto a fudge graham cookie and top with another. Eat quickly!

Variations: For s'more fun, try different types of cookies, including cinnamon grahams, fudge-covered mint cookies or gingersnaps. To add flavoring to your marshmallow, try cutting a small slit and inserting mini peanut butter cups, Rolos, M&Ms, cut-up Snickers bars or other candies. You can also squeeze in a shot of flavored Italian syrups using a small kitchen squeeze bottle for strawberry, vanilla, orange or any other flavor.

Overnight Camping Menu

Dinner
Zip Bag Salad
Pizza Pitas with
   Garlic Bread
Baked Caramel Apples
Simple S'mores

Breakfast
Brown Bag Campfire
   Breakfast
Cinnamon Twirlers
Hot Cocoa
Orange Juice

Lunch
Campfire Nachos
Sliced Fruit
Fruit Punch

Temperature of a Cooking Fire

Old-timers and mountain men could easily tell the temperature of cooking coals by holding a hand above the fire. While cooking over a fire takes practice, here is a suggested guideline to estimate the temperature of a fire. Most people can hold their hands for about 2 seconds 3–4 inches above the coals of a high-temperature fire, which is above 400 degrees F. On average, a person can hold a hand above medium-hot coals of about 350 degrees F for 4 seconds, while 6 seconds is an indicator of low-heat coals of 300 degrees F or less. The color of the coals is also an indicator of temperature. More orange signals a higher temperature and more grey-and-white ash indicates a lower temperature. Most foods cooked directly on the coals in foil do well at medium to low heat to prevent charring, while direct grilling for steaks and chops requires higher temperatures.

Camp Cleanup

Besides making camping more pleasant, a clean camp is important for health reasons. Wash hands frequently with biodegradable soap, although take care if washing with non-drinkable water such as what you might find in a stream or lake. Never use soap directly in natural waterways. A well-equipped camp kitchen should include an alcohol-based waterless hand sanitizer to be used after washing with water. Allow the hand sanitizer to evaporate before handling food to prevent unpleasant tastes from transferring.

It's also important to establish a dishwashing procedure that sanitizes dishes and utensils. A simple setup uses 2 portable washbasins. Scrape off all food residue and wash dishes in hot, soapy water in the first washbasin. In the second rinse basin, add 1 ounce (2 tablespoons) of Clorox per $2^1/2$ gallons of water to sanitize. Rinse the dishes and dry.

Wrapping Foods in Aluminum Foil

Foods cooked in aluminum foil do best when steam and heat is kept inside the foil packet. A simple, time-tested way to wrap foods in foil is to use the butcher wrap. Heavy-duty aluminum foil is less likely to be punctured when placed in a fire, while 18-inch-wide foil is easier to wrap.

1. Place the food in the center of a rectangular foil, shiny side up.

2. Bring the long sides of the foil together into the center and begin folding down, making 4–5 folds to seal (left).

3. Fold each of the short side ends over each other 4–5 times, meeting the food in the center (right).

4. Place the sealed foil packet seam side down on a second sheet of aluminum foil and repeat to have a double layer for an extra-secure wrap.

Large Group
Cooking

For really experiencing a change of pace from the modern world, there is no better way than extended camping, whether it's at a scout summer camp or on a family vacation. For youth groups and troops, this also means feeding a lot of hungry campers as deliciously and easily as possible. Camp stoves running on propane are best for large-scale kitchen operations. These recipes are designed to scale up from 12 to 100 or even more to fit your group size. Keep in mind you might need to cook in batches and plan on additional equipment and cooks.

Giant "Omelets"

12 Servings

1 stick butter
3 dozen eggs, beaten
3/4 cup milk
1/2 teaspoon
  black pepper
3/4 teaspoon salt
1 pound chopped ham
1 onion, diced
2 green bell
  peppers, diced
1 pound shredded
  cheddar jack cheese

25 Servings

2 sticks butter
6 dozen eggs, beaten
1 1/2 cups milk
1 teaspoon black
  pepper
1 1/2 teaspoons salt
2 pounds chopped ham
2 onions, diced
4 green bell
  peppers, diced
2 pounds shredded
  cheddar jack cheese

50 Servings

4 sticks butter
12 dozen eggs, beaten
3 cups milk
2 teaspoons black
  pepper
1 tablespoon salt
4 pounds chopped ham
4 onions, diced
8 green bell
  peppers, diced
4 pounds shredded
  cheddar jack cheese

Equipment

Camp stove
Large griddle

1. Preheat the griddle over medium heat, melting the butter on griddle. Combine milk with beaten eggs and mix well. Add black pepper and salt.

2. Add ham, onion and bell pepper to the hot griddle, cooking for 3–5 minutes, until onions are translucent. Pour egg mixture over the ham mixture and let cook for 3–4 minutes, until set. Cut into sections and turn over as needed to cook the other side. A large recipe may need to be cooked in batches.

3. The last few minutes, top with shredded cheese, cooking to melt.

Irish Breakfast

12 Servings

1 pound bacon
2 pounds link sausage
6 cups fresh sliced
  mushrooms
1 (32-ounce) package
  frozen hash browns,
  southern-style or
  cube, thawed
2 dozen eggs, beaten
3 small tomatoes,
  sliced
1/2 teaspoon ground
  black pepper
1 teaspoon salt

25 Servings

2 pound bacon
4 pounds link sausage
2 pounds fresh
  sliced mushrooms
2 (32-ounce) packages
  frozen hash browns,
  southern-style or
  cube, thawed
4 dozen eggs, beaten
6 tomatoes, sliced
1 teaspoon ground
  black pepper
2 teaspoons salt

50 Servings

4 pounds bacon
8 pounds link sausage
4 pounds fresh
  sliced mushrooms
2 (64-ounce) packages
  frozen hash browns,
  southern-style or
  cube, thawed
8 dozen eggs, beaten
12 tomatoes, sliced
2 teaspoons ground
  black pepper
4 teaspoons salt

Equipment

Camp stove
Large griddle

1. Cook bacon and sausage together on griddle until done. Cut sausage and bacon into bite-size pieces. Set aside and drain off most of the grease. Cook sliced mushrooms until soft and set aside.

2. Add frozen hash browns and cook, turning frequently until browned.

3. Return the sausage and bacon pieces and the sautéed mushrooms to the griddle with the hash browns. Push aside, making room to pour the egg mixture onto the griddle. Occasionally gently fold the eggs over to cook instead of chopping. As the eggs start to set, begin mixing into the hash brown mixture.

4. Add the sliced tomatoes, cooking briefly until warmed. Season with black pepper and salt.

Stovetop Soda Bread

12 Servings

6 cups all-
  purpose flour
$1^1/2$ teaspoons salt
1 tablespoon
  baking soda
3 cups buttermilk
  or $^3/_4$ cup
  buttermilk powder
  and 3 cups water

25 Servings

12 cups all-
  purpose flour
1 tablespoon salt
3 tablespoons
  baking soda
$1^1/2$ quarts buttermilk
  or $1^1/2$ cups
  buttermilk powder
  and 6 cups water

50 Servings

6 pounds plus 2 cups
  all-purpose flour
2 tablespoons salt
$^1/_3$ cup baking soda
3 quarts buttermilk
  or 3 cups buttermilk
  powder and 3 quarts
  water

Equipment

Camp stove
Large, deep, heavy
  skillet (large
  recipe may require
  several skillets)

1. Mix dry ingredients together well in a bowl and add the buttermilk. Knead lightly with floured hands. Preheat a heavy skillet over the stove on medium heat.

2. Form the dough into a flat circle the size of the skillet about $^1/2$ inch thick. Sprinkle flour into the preheated skillet and add the dough. Quickly score the top of the dough into 4 quarters with a knife.

3. Cook the bread for 6–8 minutes per side until golden brown and serve with butter, jam and honey. For large quantities, rounds of dough can be cooked on a griddle.

French Toast Casserole

12 Servings

1 stick butter
2 dozen eggs, beaten
1 pint half and half
3/4 tablespoon
  vanilla extract
6 tablespoons sugar
12 slices cooked
  bacon, crumbled
24 slices hearty
  bread, cut into
  1-inch sections
  lengthwise
Powdered sugar
Maple syrup

25 Servings

2 sticks butter
4 dozen eggs, beaten
1 quart half and half
1 1/2 tablespoons
  vanilla extract
3/4 cup sugar
1 pound cooked
  bacon, crumbled
3 loaves hearty sliced
  bread, cut into
  1-inch sections
  lengthwise
Powdered sugar
Maple syrup

50 Servings

4 sticks butter
8 dozen eggs, beaten
2 quarts half and half
3 tablespoons
  vanilla extract
1 1/2 cups sugar
2 pounds cooked
  bacon, crumbled
6 loaves hearty sliced
  bread, cut into
  1-inch sections
  lengthwise
Powdered sugar
Maple syrup

Equipment

Camp stove
Large, deep, heavy
  skillet (large
  recipe may require
  several skillets)

1. In a large skillet over medium heat, melt the butter. Mix together eggs, half and half, vanilla, sugar and crumbled bacon, beating until well blended. Place strips of bread in skillet and pour egg mixture over the bread.

2. Cook over medium heat for 8–10 minutes until bottom browns and eggs begin to set. Flip over in sections and cook another 4–5 minutes. Serve with powdered sugar and maple syrup.

Pumpkin Spiced Pancakes

12 Servings

1 (29-ounce) can
  pumpkin
6 cups pancake mix
4 cups cold water
3 teaspoons pumpkin
  pie spice
Maple syrup

25 Servings

2 (29-ounce)
  cans pumpkin
12 cups pancake mix
2 quarts cold water
2 tablespoons pumpkin
  pie spice
Maple syrup

50 Servings

4 (29-ounce)
  cans pumpkin
6 pounds plus 2 cups
  pancake mix
1 gallon cold water
2 tablespoons pumpkin
  pie spice
Maple syrup

Equipment

Camp stove ·
Large griddle

1. Combine all ingredients together except syrup and mix briefly until blended.

2. Pour 5-inch pancakes onto a lightly greased griddle over medium-high heat and cook until batter starts to bubble; flip and cook other side. Serve with syrup.

Müesli

12 Servings

6 cups rolled
 oatmeal
2 (32-ounce) containers
 vanilla yogurt
3 cups blueberries
2 pints strawberries,
 sliced
6 bananas, sliced
3 apples, diced
3/4 cup chopped candied
 walnuts (optional)

25 Servings

2 1/2 pounds rolled
 oatmeal
4 (32-ounce) containers
 vanilla yogurt
2 pints blueberries
4 pints strawberries,
 sliced
4 pounds bananas,
 sliced
6 apples, diced
1 1/2 cups chopped
 candied walnuts
 (optional)

50 Servings

5 pounds rolled
 oatmeal
8 (32-ounce) containers
 vanilla yogurt
4 pints blueberries
8 pints strawberries,
 sliced
8 pounds bananas,
 sliced
12 apples, diced
1 1/2 cups chopped
 candied walnuts
 (optional)

Equipment

Large mixing bowl

In a large mixing bowl, combine all ingredients, stirring gently to coat. Serve topped with chopped candied walnuts if desired.

Forest Hot Cereal

12 Servings

1 1/2 quarts water
3/4 teaspoon salt
4 cups steel-cut or
  Irish oatmeal
1 1/2 cups brown sugar
3 Granny Smith
  apples, diced
1 1/2 cups golden
  raisins
3 teaspoons cinnamon
Half and half

25 Servings

3 quarts water
1 1/2 teaspoons salt
8 cups steel-cut or
  Irish oatmeal
3 cups brown sugar
6 Granny Smith
  apples, diced
3 cups golden raisins
1 tablespoon cinnamon
Half and half

50 Servings

6 quarts water
  (1 1/2 gallons)
1 tablespoon salt
16 cups steel-cut
  or Irish oatmeal
2 2/3 pounds brown sugar
12 Granny Smith
  apples, diced
6 cups golden raisins
2 tablespoons cinnamon
Half and half

Equipment

Camp stove
Large pot

Bring water to a boil over high heat and add salt. Add oatmeal, cooking for about 10 minutes. Cover the pot and let stand for an additional 5 minutes. Mix in brown sugar, diced apples, golden raisins and cinnamon. Serve topped with half and half.

Sub Sandwiches

12 Servings

12 large sub
  rolls, sliced
1 (15-ounce) jar
  relish sandwich
  spread
3 pounds assorted
  sliced cold cuts
24 ounces (1½ pounds)
  sliced provolone
  cheese
6 cups shredded
  iceberg lettuce
6 tomatoes, sliced
Salt
Black pepper

25 Servings

25 large sub
  rolls, sliced
2 (15-ounce) jars
  relish sandwich
  spread
6 pounds assorted
  sliced cold cuts
3 pounds sliced
  provolone cheese
12 cups shredded
  iceberg lettuce
12 tomatoes, sliced
Salt
Black pepper

50 Servings

50 large sub
  rolls, sliced
4 (15-ounce) jars
  relish sandwich
  spread
12 pounds assorted
  sliced cold cuts
6 pounds sliced
  provolone cheese
24 cups shredded
  iceberg lettuce
24 tomatoes, sliced
Salt
Black pepper

Assemble sub sandwiches by first spreading both sides of each roll with sandwich spread and then stacking meat, cheese, lettuce and tomatoes. Sprinkle with salt and black pepper to taste.

Peanut Butter Sandwich Bar

12 Servings

3 loaves white bread
1 (40-ounce) jar
  peanut butter
2 (7-ounce)
  jars whipped
  marshmallow cream
1 (26.5-ounce) jar
  Nutella hazelnut
  chocolate spread
1 (32-ounce) jar
  grape jelly
6 sliced bananas
2 thinly sliced apples
2 cups shredded
  coconut
2 cups chopped peanuts

25 Servings

6 loaves white bread
2 (40-ounce) jars
  peanut butter
4 (7-ounce)
  jars whipped
  marshmallow cream
2 (26.5-ounce) jars
  Nutella hazelnut
  chocolate spread
2 (32-ounce) jars
  grape jelly
4 pounds sliced
  bananas
4 thinly sliced apples
4 cups shredded
  coconut
4 cups chopped peanuts

50 Servings

12 loaves white bread
4 (40-ounce) jars
  peanut butter
6 (7-ounce)
  jars whipped
  marshmallow cream
4 (26.5-ounce) jars
  Nutella hazelnut
  chocolate spread
4 (32-ounce) jars
  grape jelly
8 pounds sliced
  bananas
8 thinly sliced apples
8 cups shredded
  coconut
8 cups chopped peanuts

Spread out ingredients on a table and let each guest build the perfect peanut butter sandwich.

Really Sloppy Joes

12 Servings

3 pounds lean ground beef, crumbled
2 teaspoons black pepper
2 tablespoons garlic salt
2 onions, diced
2 green bell peppers, diced
3 (10.75-ounce) cans condensed chicken gumbo soup
1/4 cup barbecue sauce
3 3/4 cups water
12 large seeded hamburger buns
Dill pickle slices

25 Servings

6 pounds lean ground beef, crumbled
4 teaspoons black pepper
4 tablespoons garlic salt
4 onions, diced
4 green bell peppers, diced
6 (10.75-ounce) cans condensed chicken gumbo soup
1/2 cup barbecue sauce
7 1/2 cups water
25 large seeded hamburger buns
Dill pickle slices

50 Servings

12 pounds lean ground beef, crumbled
3 tablespoons black pepper
1/2 cup garlic salt
8 onions, diced
8 green bell peppers, diced
12 (10.75-ounce) cans condensed chicken gumbo soup
1 cup barbecue sauce
3 3/4 quarts water
50 large seeded hamburger buns
Dill pickle slices

Equipment

Camp stove
Large, deep, heavy skillet (large recipe may require two skillets)

1. Brown the ground beef in the skillet over medium-high heat, adding black pepper and garlic salt. Add onion and green pepper, cooking until soft. Drain excess fat.

2. Stir in the chicken gumbo soup, barbecue sauce and water, continuing to simmer over low heat for about 10 minutes. Serve on buns with dill pickle slices.

Cheeseburger Stew

12 Servings

3 pounds lean ground
  beef, crumbled
3 teaspoons salt
1 1/2 teaspoons
  black pepper
3 onions, chopped
3 (26-ounce) cans
  tomato soup
3 quarts water
3 cups dried macaroni
2 (15-ounce) jars
  Cheez Whiz

25 Servings

6 pounds lean ground
  beef, crumbled
2 tablespoons salt
1 tablespoon
  black pepper
6 onions, chopped
6 (26-ounce) cans
  tomato soup
1 1/2 gallons water
6 cups dried macaroni
4 (15-ounce) jars
  Cheez Whiz

50 Servings

12 pounds lean ground
  beef, crumbled
4 tablespoons salt
2 tablespoons
  black pepper
12 onions, chopped
7 (50-ounce) cans
  tomato soup
3 gallons water
12 cups dried macaroni
1 #10 can (104-ounce)
  Cheez Whiz

Equipment

Camp stove
Large heavy pot

1. In the bottom of a large heavy pot, brown ground beef over medium-high heat, seasoning with salt and black pepper. When the meat is almost brown, add chopped onion, continuing to cook for 3–4 more minutes until translucent. Drain excess fat.

2. Add tomato soup, water and dried macaroni. Continue cooking for 10–14 more minutes until the macaroni is soft. Stir in Cheez Whiz and serve with sliced French bread.

Grilled Onion Pepper Dogs

12 Servings

24 beef hot dogs
  (3 pounds)
1/4 cup butter
3 onions, sliced
3 cups pickled sliced
  banana peppers
24 hot dog buns
Mustard
Ketchup

25 Servings

6 pounds beef hot dogs
1 stick butter
6 onions, sliced
6 cups pickled sliced
  banana peppers
50 hot dog buns
Mustard
Ketchup

50 Servings

12 pounds beef
  hot dogs
2 sticks butter
12 onions, sliced
1 (96-ounce) jar
  pickled sliced
  banana peppers
100 hot dog buns
Mustard
Ketchup

Equipment

Camp stove
Large griddle

1. Heat the griddle over medium-high heat. Slice each hot dog lengthwise down the middle and grill on the griddle 5–7 minutes, turning frequently until browned. Add butter, onion and banana peppers, and cook until the onions are soft and translucent, stirring frequently.

2. Serve dogs on buns smothered with onions and peppers. Add condiments as desired.

Irish Spaghetti

12 Servings

3 pounds uncooked
  spaghetti noodles
3 pounds lean ground
  beef, crumbled
1^1/$_2$ teaspoons
  black pepper
2 tablespoons
  garlic salt
2 onions, diced
3 (10.75-ounce) cans
  condensed tomato soup
3 (10.75-ounce) cans
  condensed cream
  of mushroom soup
1^1/$_2$ cups water
3 tablespoons Italian
  seasoning

25 Servings

6 pounds uncooked
  spaghetti noodles
6 pounds lean ground
  beef, crumbled
1 tablespoon
  black pepper
4 tablespoons
  garlic salt
4 onions, diced
6 (10.75-ounce) cans
  condensed tomato soup
6 (10.75-ounce) cans
  condensed cream
  of mushroom soup
3 cups water
^{1}/$_3$ cup Italian
  seasoning

50 Servings

12 pounds uncooked
  spaghetti noodles
12 pounds lean ground
  beef, crumbled
2 tablespoons
  black pepper
^{1}/$_2$ cup garlic salt
8 onions, diced
5 (26-ounce) family-
  size cans condensed
  tomato soup
5 (26-ounce)
  family-size cans
  condensed cream
  of mushroom soup
6 cups water
^{2}/$_3$ cup Italian
  seasoning

Equipment

Camp stove
Large pot
Large, deep, heavy
  skillet (large
  recipe may require
  2 skillets)

1. Prepare spaghetti noodles according to package instructions.

2. Brown ground beef in the skillet over medium-high heat, adding black pepper
   and garlic salt. Add the onion, cooking until soft and translucent. Drain excess
   fat. Stir in the soups, water and Italian seasoning. Bring to a simmer over low
   heat and cook for 10 minutes. Serve over hot spaghetti noodles.

Tacorittos

12 Servings

3 pounds lean ground beef, crumbled
3 packages taco seasoning
3 (15-ounce) cans pinto beans, undrained
3 (10-ounce) cans Rotel tomatoes and green peppers, undrained
24 ounces shredded Mexican-style cheese
1 regular bag nacho cheese Doritos
6 cups shredded iceberg lettuce
16 ounces sour cream

25 Servings

6 pounds lean ground beef, crumbled
1 cup taco seasoning
1 #10 can pinto beans, undrained
6 (10-ounce) cans Rotel tomatoes and green peppers, undrained
3 pounds shredded Mexican-style cheese
2 regular bags nacho cheese Doritos
12 cups shredded iceberg lettuce
32 ounces sour cream

50 Servings

12 pounds lean ground beef, crumbled
2 cups taco seasoning
2 #10 cans pinto beans, undrained
12 (10-ounce) cans Rotel tomatoes and green peppers, undrained
6 pounds shredded Mexican-style cheese
4 regular bags nacho cheese Doritos
24 cups shredded iceberg lettuce
64 ounces sour cream

Equipment

Camp stove
Large, deep, heavy skillet (large recipe may require 2 skillets)

1. Brown ground beef in the skillet over medium-high heat. Drain excess fat. Add taco seasoning, pinto beans and tomatoes. Continue simmering for 8–10 minutes to reduce liquid.

2. Stir in shredded cheese and Doritos until cheese is melted. Serve with shredded lettuce and sour cream.

For a Navajo taco variation, make the recipe without adding Doritos and serve over scones with lettuce, salsa and sour cream.

Beef Goulash

12 Servings

2¹/₂ pounds uncooked
  spiral pasta
3 tablespoons
  vegetable oil
2 pounds flank steak,
  cut into strips
2 teaspoons salt
3 teaspoons black
  pepper
3 teaspoons
  garlic powder
2 large onions,
  chopped
2 red bell peppers,
  chopped
¹/₃ cup all-
  purpose flour
3 (14.5-ounce) cans
  diced tomatoes,
  undrained
3 (14-ounce) cans
  beef broth
3 teaspoons paprika

25 Servings

5 pounds uncooked
  spiral pasta
¹/₃ cup vegetable oil
6 pounds flank steak,
  cut into strips
1¹/₂ tablespoons salt
2 tablespoons
  black pepper
2 tablespoons
  garlic powder
4 large onions,
  chopped
4 red bell peppers,
  chopped
1 cup all-
  purpose flour
6 (14.5-ounce) cans
  diced tomatoes,
  undrained
3 (32-ounce) cartons
  beef broth
2 tablespoons paprika

50 Servings

10 pounds uncooked
  spiral pasta
²/₃ cup vegetable oil
12 pounds flank steak,
  cut into strips
3 tablespoons salt
4 tablespoons
  black pepper
4 tablespoons
  garlic powder
8 large onions,
  chopped
8 red bell peppers,
  chopped
2 cups all-
  purpose flour
12 (14.5-ounce) cans
  diced tomatoes,
  undrained
6 (32-ounce) cartons
  beef broth
4 tablespoons paprika

Equipment

Camp stove
Large, deep, heavy
  skillet or Dutch oven
  (large recipe may
  require 2 skillets)

1. Prepare pasta according to package directions. In a large skillet, heat oil over medium-high heat, adding steak strips, salt, black pepper and garlic powder. Cook for 5–6 minutes until brown. Add onion and red bell peppers, and continue to cook until slightly softened.

2. Add flour to oil and drippings in the skillet and stir until a smooth paste is formed. Add remaining ingredients and continue simmering on low heat for 8–10 more minutes. Serve over drained pasta.

Cheese 'n' Mac

12 Servings

48 ounces (3 pounds)
  uncooked large
  elbow macaroni
1¹/2 cups butter
1 (28-ounce) can
  petite-diced
  tomatoes, undrained
24 ounces (1¹/2 pounds)
  shredded Mexican-
  style cheese blend
³/4 teaspoons ground
  black pepper
Salt to taste

25 Servings

6 pounds uncooked
  large elbow macaroni
6 sticks butter
2 (28-ounce) can
  petite-diced
  tomatoes, undrained
3 pounds shredded
  Mexican-style
  cheese blend
1¹/2 teaspoons ground
  black pepper
Salt to taste

25 Servings

12 pounds uncooked
  large elbow macaroni
6 sticks butter
4 (28-ounce) cans
  petite-diced
  tomatoes, undrained
6 pounds shredded
  Mexican-style
  cheese blend
1¹/2 teaspoons ground
  black pepper
Salt to taste

Equipment

Camp stove
Large heavy pot

In a large pot, boil the macaroni covered with at least 3 inches of water until tender and then drain. Keeping the macaroni hot in the pot over low heat, add butter, tomatoes, shredded cheese, black pepper and salt. Serve immediately.

Chicken and Dumplings

12 Servings

3 cups biscuit mix
(Bisquick)
1 cup milk
3 tablespoons olive
or vegetable oil
1 pound baby carrots
12 boneless skinless
chicken breasts
(4 pounds)
3 (10.75-ounce) cans
condensed cream
of chicken soup
3 (10.75-ounce) cans
condensed golden
mushroom soup
1 1/2 cups water
3 (4-ounce) cans
mushrooms, drained

25 Servings

6 cups biscuit mix
(Bisquick)
2 cups milk
1/3 cup olive or
vegetable oil
2 pounds baby carrots
25 boneless skinless
chicken breasts
(8 pounds)
3 (26-ounce)
family-size cans
condensed cream
of chicken soup
5 (10.75-ounce) cans
condensed golden
mushroom soup
3 cups water
6 (4-ounce) cans
mushrooms, drained

50 Servings

12 cups biscuit
mix (Bisquick)
1 quart milk
2/3 cup olive or
vegetable oil
4 pounds baby carrots
50 boneless skinless
chicken breasts
(16 pounds)
2 (50-ounce) cans
condensed cream
of chicken soup
12 (10.75-ounce) cans
condensed golden
mushroom soup
1 1/2 quarts water
1 #10 can mushrooms,
drained

Equipment

Camp stove
Large, deep, heavy
lidded skillet
or Dutch oven
(large recipe may
require several
large skillets or
roasting pans)

1. Mix biscuit mix and milk to form a soft dough and set aside.

2. In a heavy skillet, heat the oil over medium-high heat. Add carrots and chicken breasts, cooking for 6 minutes, turning often to brown. Add soups, water and mushrooms, bringing mixture to a simmer. Drop large spoonfuls of dough onto the chicken and vegetables to form dumplings. Cover and continue cooking 15–20 more minutes until dumplings are done.

No Fridge
Fruit Salad

12 Servings

1 (20-ounce) can
  crushed pineapple
4 (15-ounce) cans
  mandarin oranges,
  undrained
2 large boxes instant
  lemon pudding
2 (29-ounce) cans
  sliced peaches,
  drained
10–12 bananas sliced
  (4 pounds)
3 cups mini
  marshmallows
3/4 cups chopped
  pecans (optional)

25 Servings

2 (20-ounce) cans
  crushed pineapple
8 (15-ounce) cans
  mandarin oranges
4 large boxes instant
  lemon pudding
4 (29-ounce) cans
  sliced peaches,
  drained
8 pounds bananas,
  sliced
1 (1-pound) package
  mini marshmallows
1 1/2 cups chopped
  pecans (optional)

50 Servings

4 (20-ounce) cans
  crushed pineapple
16 (15-ounce) cans
  mandarin oranges,
  undrained
8 large boxes instant
  lemon pudding
8 (29-ounce) cans
  sliced peaches,
  drained
16 pounds bananas,
  sliced
2 (1-pound) packages
  mini marshmallows
3 cups chopped
  pecans (optional)

Drain juice from the pineapple and mandarin oranges into a large bowl. Stir in lemon pudding and whisk to blend well. Add the fruit and marshmallows and stir gently to combine. Fold in chopped pecans if desired.

Scones

12 Servings

1¹/₂ cups sugar
3 packages
  yeast (about
  2¹/₂ tablespoons)
4¹/₂ cups milk,
  warmed to about
  105 degrees F
11 cups (3 pounds)
  all-purpose flour
3 teaspoons salt
Vegetable oil
  for frying
1 pound butter
16 ounces honey

25 Servings

3 cups sugar
6 packages dry yeast
  (¹/₃ cup dry yeast)
1 quart plus 1 cup
  milk, warmed to
  about 105 degrees F
6 pounds all-
  purpose flour
2 tablespoons salt
Vegetable oil
  for frying
2 pounds butter
32 ounces honey

50 Servings

6 cups sugar
²/₃ cup dry yeast
2¹/₂ quarts milk,
  warmed to about
  105 degrees F
12 pounds all-
  purpose flour
4 tablespoons salt
Vegetable oil
  for frying
4 pounds butter
64 ounces honey

Equipment

Camp stove
Large, deep, heavy
  skillet or Dutch oven
  (large recipe may
  require 2 skillets)

1. Dissolve sugar and yeast into warm milk. Let stand for about 5 minutes to activate. Combine flour and salt in a large mixing bowl. Create a well in the top of the flour and pour in milk mixture while stirring. Continue stirring and kneading until a soft dough forms. If the mixture is too sticky to shape by hand, add flour little by little. Cover bowl and let sit 10 minutes in a warm area.

2. Heat the oil in a heavy skillet on medium high until hot. If the oil smokes, it is too hot. By hand, pull balls of dough out of the bowl and stretch into a scone shape about ¹/₂-inch thick. Fry in the oil, turning once until golden on both sides. Place on paper towels to drain. Serve with butter and honey or make Navajo Tacos with Tacoritto (see page 49) meat mixture.

Easy Slaw

12 Servings

1¹/2 cups mayonnaise
¹/3 cup sugar
¹/4 cup cider vinegar
24 ounces shredded
  cabbage
¹/2 teaspoon
  celery seed
¹/2 teaspoon salt
¹/2 teaspoon
  black pepper

25 Servings

3 cups mayonnaise
²/3 cup sugar
¹/2 cup cider vinegar
48 ounces shredded
  cabbage
1 teaspoon celery seed
1 teaspoon salt
1 teaspoon black
  pepper

50 Servings

6 cups mayonnaise
1¹/3 cups sugar
1 cup cider vinegar
96 ounces shredded
  cabbage
2 teaspoons
  celery seed
2 teaspoons salt
2 teaspoons black
  pepper

Mix all ingredients together in a large bowl and serve.

Summer Camp Menu

Day 1
Lunch: Sub
  Sandwiches,
  Potato Chips
Dinner: Zip Bag
  Salad, Irish
  Spaghetti,
  Pumpernickel
  Bread, Simple
  S'mores

Day 2
Breakfast: Müesli
Lunch: Grilled
  Onion Dogs,
  Multi-Grain Chips
Dinner: Chicken
  and Dumplings,
  No Fridge Fruit
  Salad, Soda
  Pop Cobbler

Day 3
Breakfast: Irish
  Breakfast
Lunch: Cheese 'n'
  Mac, Crackers,
  Sliced Fresh
  Vegetables
Dinner: Really
  Sloppy Joes,
  Easy Slaw, Baked
  Caramel Apples

Day 4
Breakfast: French
  Toast Casserole
Lunch: Campfire
  Nachos, Green
  Salad
Dinner:
  Tacorittos,
  Scones

Day 5
Breakfast: Pumpkin
  Spice Pancakes
Lunch: Peanut
  Butter Sandwich
  Bar, Vegetable
  Chips
Dinner: Beef
  Goulash, French
  Bread, Cinnamon
  Twirlers,
  Banana Boats

Day 6
Breakfast: Forest
  Hot Cereal

Camp Cooking Duties

While scouts and youth groups understand the importance of a duty roster on a
camping trip to distribute camp cooking responsibilities equally, having either a formal
or informal system of dividing duties can also be helpful for families and groups of
friends. Equally dividing kitchen jobs not only ensures that one person isn't overly
burdened, but it also gives everyone an opportunity to experience the fun in cooking
outdoors. While organized groups may find it necessary to maintain a schedule that
allows for an equal rotation, less formal methods may include assigning a member of
the party to make sure tasks are divided evenly.

Choosing an Expedition Stove

Efficient cooking for more than 2 people requires a larger expedition camp stove with 2 or more burners. The most common types of stoves are fueled by propane or liquid white gas. A propane camp stove is the most similar to a standard natural gas home range. It has the advantage of being easy to operate. Simply turn the burner adjustment and light. Propane stoves also can offer more room for cooking, extra burners and often are self-supported at waist level. Many manufacturers make integrated griddles or even smoke boxes for grilling burgers and meat. Propane stoves have the disadvantage of usually being larger and heavier than white gas stoves. Many also require full-size LP tanks similar to a gas grill, which take up space and can be heavy.

White gas camp stoves tend to be smaller and lighter, which is nice if you have limited packing space. Liquid fuels are also easy to refuel while camping, which can be a benefit. While both types of stoves perform more poorly at altitude and low temperatures, white gas generally produces more heat than comparable propane stoves in adverse conditions. Liquid fuel stoves tend to be more difficult to operate. It's important to learn how to use the stove before the trip begins.

Camp Kitchen Essential Tools

While camping requires a certain amount of learning how to make do without conveniences found in a home kitchen, taking time to assemble a few essential tools can make life a lot easier in the field. An easy way to keep implements accessible is to store them in a fabric shoe hanger or a specialized camp-cooking organizer. Roll up the storage hanger and place it in a plastic storage bin with pots, pans and other gear. This list may be helpful for stocking your kitchen:

Chief's knife

Small knife

Plastic cutting board

Pancake turner

Wire whisk

Large serving and mixing spoon

Ladle

Large mixing bowl

Small mixing bowl

Can opener

Vegetable peeler

Measuring spoons

Measuring cups

Wash basins (2)

Biodegradable dish soap

Small bottle of liquid bleach (for sanitizing)

Dutch
Oven

The Dutch oven is the original way to cook while camping, even when
the early pioneers and settlers didn't know they were camping!
With a Dutch oven, an entirely new world of hearty eating opens up.
Foods can be baked with dry heat or braised with moisture,
while the larger size of a Dutch oven makes it easy to cook enough
food for most groups at one time. The basics of Dutch oven cooking
can be mastered with a little practice and a healthy appetite.

Incredible Breakfast Pie

Serves 6-8

1 refrigerated pie
  crust (or 1 package
  pie crust mix
  prepared according
  to directions)
8 slices cooked
  bacon, crumbled
1 cup shredded
  cheddar cheese
1¹/₂ cups milk

¹/₂ cup all-
  purpose flour
1 teaspoon salt
2 green onions,
  finely diced
1 tablespoon fresh
  or dried parsley
8 eggs, beaten
Ketchup or salsa

Equipment

Parchment paper
Charcoal briquettes
  or campfire coals
10-inch Dutch oven,
  8 coals on bottom,
  14 coals on top,
  350 degrees F

1. Line the bottom of a 10-inch Dutch oven with strips of folded baking parchment up the side of the oven to aid in removing the pie. Unroll the pie crust and place in the bottom of the oven, stretching up the sides. Pinch edges between thumb and forefinger to scallop.

2. Sprinkle bacon and cheese on the bottom of the pie crust. Add milk, flour, salt, green onions and parsley to the beaten eggs and mix well. Pour egg mixture into the pie crust.

3. Cover and bake with heat on top and bottom for 45 minutes until eggs are set. Allow cooling for 10 minutes before lifting out the pie. Serve with ketchup or salsa.

Egg Strata

Serves 6–8

10 slices hearty
   white bread (stale
   bread works well)
1/4 cup butter,
   softened
8 ounces shredded
   Mexican-style cheese
12 eggs beaten
2 cups half and half
2 cups milk

2 teaspoons salt
1/2 teaspoon ground
   black pepper
1/4 teaspoon paprika
1 tablespoon prepared
   yellow mustard
1 teaspoon
   Worcestershire sauce
2 cups chopped
   mushrooms

Equipment

Charcoal briquettes
   or campfire coals
12-inch Dutch oven,
   10 coals on bottom,
   16 coals on top,
   350 degrees F

1. Butter one side of each bread slice. Cut bread slices into fourths. Layer half the bread in the bottom of a Dutch oven, butter side down. Sprinkle with half of the cheese. Layer the remaining bread on top and sprinkle with the rest of the cheese.

2. Combine the remaining ingredients and mix well. Pour egg mixture over bread. Cover and place in the cooler for at least 2 hours and preferably overnight.

3. Bake with heat on top and bottom for 1 hour covered. Let stand 10 minutes before slicing and serving.

Quick Cinnamon Rolls

Serves 6-8

1 loaf frozen bread
dough, thawed
(substitute Outback
Roll dough (page 79)
if you prefer to
make from scratch)

1 stick butter, melted
1 cup brown sugar
1 teaspoon cinnamon
$1/2$ cup chopped pecans
1 cup raisins
(optional)

Equipment

Parchment paper
Charcoal briquettes
or campfire coals
12-inch Dutch oven,
10 coals on bottom,
16 coals on top,
350 degrees F

Glaze

2 cups powdered sugar
2-4 tablespoons milk

$1/2$ teaspoon vanilla
extract

1. Roll out bread dough lengthwise on a sheet of baking parchment or wax paper until it is about 10 inches wide by 20 inches long. Spread with melted butter, sugar, cinnamon, pecans and raisins, if desired. Roll up from the long edge and cut rolls into sections every $1^1/2$ inches.

2. Place in a greased Dutch oven and allow to rise in a warm area for about 1 hour. Bake with heat on top and bottom for 20–25 minutes.

3. Prepare glaze by whisking powdered sugar, milk and vanilla, adding more milk 1 tablespoon at a time to reach desired consistency. Drizzle over hot cinnamon rolls and serve.

Berry Breakfast

Serves 6–8

2 cups all-
  purpose flour
2 eggs, beaten
1 teaspoon baking
  powder
1 cup sour cream
1/2 teaspoon
  baking soda
1/2 cup sugar

1/2 cup butter, melted
1 cup raspberries
  or boysenberries
3/4 cup brown sugar
Boysenberry
  pancake syrup
Whipped cream
  (optional)

Equipment

Charcoal briquettes
  or campfire coals
12-inch Dutch oven,
  10 coals on bottom,
  16 coals on top,
  350 degrees F

Combine all ingredients in a mixing bowl except berries and brown sugar and mix until moist throughout. Gently fold in the berries and pour into a 12-inch Dutch oven. Top with brown sugar. Bake with heat on top and bottom for 40 minutes. Serve warm with boysenberry syrup and whipped cream.

Dutch Oven Potatoes

Serves 6–8

1 stick butter
1/2 cup water
2 tablespoons fresh
  or dried parsley
1 tablespoon chopped
  rosemary

1/2 teaspoon
  black pepper
12 red potatoes,
  quartered
1 small onion, diced

Equipment

Charcoal briquettes
  or campfire coals
12-inch Dutch oven,
  10 coals on bottom,
  16 coals on top,
  350 degrees F

1. Heat Dutch oven over coals, adding butter to melt. Add water, herbs and black pepper. Stir in potatoes and onions and evenly coat.

2. Cover and cook for 45 minutes with heat on top and bottom, stirring halfway through until potatoes are tender and brown.

Curry Chicken

Serves 6–8

1 tablespoon olive
   or vegetable oil
1¹/₂ pounds chicken
   breast, cut
   into strips
2 (13.5-ounce) cans
   coconut milk
4–6 tablespoons
   yellow curry paste,
   or to taste
1 (8-ounce) can bamboo
   shoots, drained

1 (8-ounce) package
   frozen peas
   and carrots
¹/₂ cup fresh basil
   (substitute
   2 tablespoons
   dried basil)
2 potatoes, cubed
5 cups water
2 cups uncooked
   white rice

Equipment

Charcoal briquettes
   or campfire coals
12-inch Dutch oven,
   8 coals on bottom,
   14 coals on top,
   325 degrees F

1. Heat Dutch oven over coals and add oil. Add chicken strips, cooking about 5 minutes while stirring to brown. Add additional ingredients and stir to mix well.

2. Cover and cook for 35–45 minutes with heat on top and bottom, until rice has absorbed much of the liquid.

Biscuits and Gravy

Serves 6–8

3 cups biscuit mix
  (Bisquick)
3 cups milk, divided
1 pound ground
  breakfast sausage
2 tablespoons dried
  onion flakes

4 tablespoons flour
2 cubes chicken
  bouillon
1 teaspoon ground
  black pepper

Equipment

Parchment paper
Charcoal briquettes
  or campfire coals
12-inch Dutch oven,
  10 coals on bottom,
  16 coals on top,
  350 degrees F

1. Mix biscuit mix with 1 cup of milk, reserving 2 cups. Roll out dough on a floured surface and cut out biscuits with a glass or biscuit cutter. Place in a Dutch oven that has been prepared with folded strips of baking parchment so that biscuits can easily be removed.

2. Bake for 10–15 minutes until golden brown with heat on top and bottom. Remove biscuits and return Dutch oven to the fire without the lid.

3. Brown sausage with onion flakes until cooked. Drain off most of the fat, reserving a few tablespoons in the Dutch oven. Add flour slowly while stirring to make a smooth paste. Add 2 cups of milk and almost bring to a boil. Add chicken bouillon and ground black pepper and cook for about 5 minutes. Thin, if necessary, with additional milk. Serve sausage gravy over biscuits.

Lemon-Lime Turkey Steak

Serves 6-8

6-8 turkey breast
  steaks (about
  2 pounds)
1 (12-ounce) can
  lemon-lime soda
2 tablespoons
  lemon juice
2 tablespoons
  soy sauce

2 tablespoons
  melted butter
1 teaspoon ginger
Hot prepared rice
  (optional)

Equipment

Charcoal briquettes
  or campfire coals
12-inch Dutch oven,
  10 coals on bottom,
  16 coals on top,
  350 degrees F

1. Place all ingredients in a gallon-size Ziploc freezer bag and marinate for at least 4 hours or overnight.

2. When ready to cook, pour contents from the freezer bag into a 12-inch Dutch oven and cook with heat on top and bottom for 30 minutes. Serve over rice or with Dutch Oven Potatoes (see page 70).

Icebox Cooking Method

An easy way to minimize the amount of time spent preparing food on a campout is to prepare ingredients at home and package in gallon-size Ziploc bags. Store the bags of ingredients in an ice chest, ready to be combined to make recipes. This method works especially well for Dutch oven dishes. Many ingredients can be frozen beforehand in Ziploc bags and placed in the cooler to help maintain a safe temperature for refrigerated foods. It's also often easy to precook ground beef mixtures at home and bring them refrigerated or frozen. Recipes in this cookbook that are well suited to the icebox method of preparation are marked with a special symbol.

Fireman Enchiladas

Serves 6–8

1 pound ground beef
1 small onion, chopped
2 bell peppers, green
   or red, chopped
1 (4-ounce) can diced
   green chilies
1 (10-ounce) can
   enchilada sauce
3 (15.5-ounce)
   cans pinto beans,
   undrained

2 (28-ounce) cans
   diced tomatoes
1 (4.25-ounce) can
   sliced olives
6–8 flour tortillas
3 cups shredded
   cheddar cheese
Sour cream

Equipment

Charcoal briquettes
   or campfire coals
12-inch Dutch oven,
   10 coals on bottom,
   16 coals on top,
   350 degrees F

1. Heat Dutch oven over coals and brown ground beef with onion until cooked through. Drain excess fat. Add remaining ingredients except for tortillas, cheese and sour cream. Simmer for about 10 minutes and remove to a separate bowl.

2. To assemble enchiladas, dip each tortilla in the mixture's sauce to coat. Fill with meat and beans and roll up, placing each enchilada back into the Dutch oven. Top with cheese. Bake with heat on top and bottom for about 30–40 minutes until hot throughout. Serve with sour cream.

Pioneer Pizza

Serves 6–8

2 tablespoons
  corn meal
1 loaf frozen bread
  dough, thawed
  (substitute Outback
  Roll dough, page 79)
1 (10-ounce) bottle
  barbecue sauce
16 ounces shredded
  mozzarella or pizza
  blend cheese

1 (8-ounce) package
  cooked, sliced
  chicken breast
1 small red
  onion, diced
1/2 cup fresh cilantro,
  loosely chopped

Equipment

Charcoal briquettes
  or campfire coals
12-inch Dutch oven,
  14 coals on bottom,
  16 coals on top,
  400 degrees F

1. Sprinkle cornmeal in the bottom of a 12-inch or larger Dutch oven. Roll or stretch out bread dough to fit the bottom of the Dutch oven and set in place.

2. Spread barbecue sauce on dough, followed by cheese, chicken, red onion and fresh cilantro. Bake with heat on top and bottom for 15–20 minutes.

Smoky Brisket

Serves 6–8

1 package dry
  onion soup mix
1 (12-ounce) jar
  chili sauce
1 (12-ounce) can
  regular Dr. Pepper

$^1/_4$ teaspoon natural
  liquid smoke
1 (4–5 pound)
  beef brisket

Equipment

Charcoal briquettes
  or campfire coals
12-inch Dutch oven,
  10 coals on bottom,
  16 coals on top,
  350 degrees F

In a bowl, combine all ingredients except brisket. Place brisket fat side up in a Dutch oven and pour sauce over the top. Bake with heat on top and bottom for 45 minutes per pound of meat. Every hour or so, you may need to restock with hot coals.

Cowboy Beans

Serves 6-8

8 slices bacon
1 tablespoon flour
1 small onion, chopped
2 (15.5-ounce) cans
    pinto beans

2 (15.5-ounce) cans
    kidney beans
2 pints chicken stock
$1/2$ teaspoon sage
$1/2$ teaspoon thyme

Equipment

Charcoal briquettes
    or campfire coals
12-inch Dutch oven,
    18 coals on bottom,
    no coals on top,
    350 degrees F

1. Heat Dutch oven over coals and fry bacon until cooked and then crumble; drain off grease, reserving 1–2 tablespoons in the oven. Add flour and stir to form a smooth paste, cooking until light brown. Add onions and cook 3 more minutes until translucent.

2. Add remaining ingredients and continue simmering covered for another 30 minutes until thickened.

Outback Rolls

Serves 6-8

1/4 cup butter
1/4 cup water
1 cup milk
1/3 cup sugar
1 package yeast

2 eggs, beaten
1 teaspoon salt
4 1/2 cups flour

Equipment

Small saucepan
Charcoal briquettes
  or campfire coals
12-inch Dutch oven,
  14 coals on bottom,
  20 coals on top,
  450 degrees F

1. Melt butter in a small saucepan. Add water, milk and sugar, continuing to cook until warm, about 105 degrees F. Remove from heat and add yeast. Wait for 5–10 minutes for yeast to activate and foam. Add eggs and stir.

2. In a large mixing bowl, combine salt and flour. Add the liquid ingredients and stir to create a soft dough. Knead for 5 minutes and cover. Allow to rise for 20 minutes in a warm place.

3. Punch down dough and form into 18–20 balls. Place in a warm Dutch oven and allow to rise for 20 minutes. Bake with heat on top and bottom for 15–18 minutes. Brush tops with butter while warm.

Rocky Mountain Meatballs

Serves 6–8

2 pounds ground beef
1 envelope dry
   onion soup mix
1/2 cup cracker crumbs
3 eggs, beaten
1 tablespoon
   vegetable oil
1 small onion, sliced

4 large potatoes,
   sliced into rounds
2 (10.75-ounce) cans
   condensed cream
   of mushroom soup
2 cups sour cream
Salt
Ground black pepper

Equipment

Charcoal briquettes
   or campfire coals
12-inch Dutch oven,
   10 coals on bottom,
   16 coals on top,
   350 degrees F

1. Combine ground beef, soup mix, cracker crumbs and eggs, mixing well. Form into 2-inch balls. Heat oil in a Dutch oven until hot, add onions and meatballs, cooking until the outsides of the meatballs are brown and onions are softened.

2. Drain excess oil. Add potatoes and cover with mushroom soup and sour cream, stirring to coat. Season with salt and black pepper to taste. Bake with heat on top and bottom for 45 minutes.

Pumpkin Cobbler

Serves 6–8

1 (30-ounce) can
  pumpkin
1 cup sugar
3 eggs, beaten
2 teaspoons pumpkin
  pie spice
3/4 teaspoon salt
1 (12-ounce) can
  evaporated milk

1/2 cup butter, melted
1 box yellow cake mix
1/2 cup chopped
  pecans (optional)
Whipped cream or
  ice cream

Equipment

Charcoal briquettes
  or campfire coals
12-inch Dutch oven,
  10 coals on bottom,
  16 coals on top,
  350 degrees F

1. In a Dutch oven, combine pumpkin, sugar, eggs, spice, salt and milk. Mix well.

2. In a small mixing bowl, use a fork to cut melted butter into the cake mix. Add pecans if desired.

3. Spread cake mix topping over pumpkin and Bake with heat on top and bottom for 50–60 minutes. Serve topped with whipped cream or ice cream.

Mountain Man Donuts

Makes about 2 dozen

1 cup boiling water
3/4 cup instant mashed
  potato flakes
3/4 cup warm milk
1 package yeast
1/4 cup melted butter
1/4 cup sugar
1 egg

1/2 teaspoon salt
4 cups flour
Vegetable oil
  for frying
2 cups powdered sugar
2-4 tablespoons water
1/2 teaspoon vanilla
  extract

Equipment

Charcoal briquettes
  or campfire coals
12-inch Dutch oven,
  12 coals on bottom,
  375 degrees F

1. In a small mixing bowl, add boiling water to potato flakes to reconstitute. In a larger mixing bowl, combine milk, yeast, butter and sugar. Allow to rest until yeast activates and turns foamy.

2. Add the egg to milk mixture, whisking to beat. Add mashed potatoes, salt and flour one cup and a time, stirring until a soft dough is formed. Dough should be soft and slightly sticky. Allow to rest covered in a warm place until double in size.

3. On a floured surface, roll out dough to 1/2 inch thickness and cut with a doughnut cutter or the top of a glass. Cut out center with a narrow bottle mouth or cap to form doughnuts.

4. Heat 2–3 inches of oil in a Dutch oven and fry doughnuts a few at a time until golden brown. Glaze with powdered sugar blended with water and vanilla extract.

Four-Day Dutch Oven Outfitter Menu

Day 1

Dinner: Curry Chicken, No Fridge Fruit Salad, Pineapple Upside Down Cake

Day 2

Breakfast: Egg Strata, Quick Cinnamon Rolls

Dinner: Smoky Brisket, Cowboy Beans, Easy Slaw, Outback Rolls, Soda Pop Cobbler

Day 3

Breakfast: Berry Breakfast, Fresh Fruit

Dinner: Fireman Enchiladas, Fresh Pico de Gallo and Iceberg Lettuce, Pumpkin Cobbler

Day 4

Breakfast: Incredible Breakfast Pie, Mountain Man Donuts

Clean-Up Tips

A well-seasoned Dutch oven should be easy to clean. Simply remove as much food residue as possible and wipe with a paper towel with a little vegetable oil. For messier clean-up jobs, add warm water with a very small amount of mild dish soap. Too much detergent can remove the seasoning that protects cast iron.

A few tips can help with clean up. Lining the bottom of the oven with strips of baking parchment paper that extends above the baked goods makes it easier to remove rolls, biscuits, cakes and pies. Aluminum foil lining used judiciously can also make clean up easier, although many times food in contact with a well-seasoned Dutch oven is more flavorful. Disposable aluminum Dutch oven liners also make clean up a snap. Whatever you do, don't forget to apply a very light coat of vegetable oil or cast iron conditioner to all surfaces of the oven while it is still warm after washing. This will prevent rust while the oven is stored.

Cast Iron Use and Care

Cast iron cookware has been valued for its cooking properties for hundreds of years. Cast iron distributes heat evenly, resulting in the unique property of being resistant to fluctuations in cooking temperature. It also is very durable, lasting for a lifetime if properly cared for.

It's important to make sure new cast iron cookware is properly seasoned. While many manufacturers offer Dutch ovens and other cookware that is already seasoned, you may find a better value in seasoning the cast iron yourself. To season cast iron, heat up the Dutch oven or skillet in a hot fire or on an outdoor gas grill until very hot. Using a paper towel or basting brush, spread vegetable oil on all surfaces. Return to the heat to burn off the oil, changing the color of the metal from light grey to the black usually associated with a Dutch oven. Remove from heat and cool. While the oven is still warm, rub in a final very light coat of vegetable oil or cast iron conditioner over all surfaces.

Pushing the Iron Envelope

After you have a little experience, push the boundaries of Dutch oven cooking by adapting recipes from home. Master Dutch oven chefs are able to create 5-course meals, all cooked in cast iron. Dutch ovens and cast iron also work great at home in the oven, allowing you to practice recipes before heading out to the wild.

You may want to add special tools to your gear, if you plan to cook in a Dutch oven frequently. A lid-removal tool is handy for quick checks on the food. A trivet lid holder allows you to present and serve your Dutch oven dish on the lid of the oven. A Dutch oven charcoal stand brings the cooking up to waist level for convenience while cooking.

For those interested in backpacking, canoe or kayak touring, or horse backing, many manufacturers sell lightweight cast aluminum Dutch ovens. A small 8-inch oven is great for short backpack trips and opens a whole range of possibilities. Aluminum also has the advantage of not needing to be seasoned.

Cooking at the Right Temperature

OVEN top/bottom	325°	350°	375°	400°	425°	450°
8-inch	15	16	17	18	19	20
*****	10/5	11/5	11/6	12/6	13/6	14/6
10-inch	19	21	23	25	27	29
*****	13/6	14/7	16/7	17/8	18/9	19/10
12-inch	23	25	27	29	31	33
*****	16/7	17/8	18/9	19/10	21/10	22/11
14-inch	30	32	34	36	38	40
*****	20/10	21/11	22/12	24/12	25/13	26/14

While you certainly can use a Dutch oven right in coals from a traditional wood campfire, most backwoods chefs find charcoal briquettes easier to use for maintaining consistent temperatures. The number of briquettes determines the temperature. Each recipe specifies how many briquettes you'll need, or refer to the chart above, provided by Lodge Cast Iron. You may find that a chimney-style briquette igniter helps you create hotter charcoal to work with much faster.

Camp Gourmet

So you've mastered camp cooking so far and are ready for hot and haute cuisine. The following recipes are designed to inspire your inner celebrity chef and allow you to show off your mastery of outdoor cooking. They will also appeal to the more discerning palates of leaders and adult groups. Allow your imagination and taste buds to lead you where they will.

Sourdough Pancakes

Serves 4

1 cup sourdough
  starter
2 cups unbleached
  all-purpose flour

1 egg, beaten
2 tablespoons sugar
$^{1}/_{2}$ teaspoon salt
2 cups buttermilk

Equipment

Camp stove
Griddle

1. Combine all ingredients in a mixing bowl and stir gently. Don't over mix. Batter should be slightly lumpy. Pour onto a lightly greased griddle heated over medium-high heat and cook pancakes, turning once bubbles have burst.

2. Serve with butter and warm maple syrup.

Variation: Mix in blueberries, diced bananas or diced apples and a pinch of cinnamon.

★★★

Sourdough Starter

Serves 4

1 package yeast
1 teaspoon sugar

2 cups warm water
2 cups flour

Dissolve yeast and sugar into the warm water. Wait 5 minutes until bubbly. Mix in flour one cup at a time until a sticky dough is formed. Place in a glass jar (not metal), cover loosely and leave out at room temperature for 3–4 days until bubbly. Refrigerate. When you use 1 cup of starter, replace with 1 cup each of water and flour and leave out at room temperature until it ferments again before refrigerating.

Sausage and Pepper Breakfast Burritos

Serves 4-6

1 pound chorizo
  sausage
2 potatoes, diced
1 red bell pepper,
  sliced

1 orange bell
  pepper, sliced
8 ounces Cotija
  cheese, crumbled
Salsa
8-10 tortillas

Equipment

Camp stove or
  campfire coals
Skillet or Dutch oven

1. Crumble sausage and cook for about 10 minutes over medium-high heat with the diced potato until sausage is brown and potato is soft. Add bell pepper slices, cooking until soft. Top with crumbled Cotija cheese and set aside, keeping warm.

2. Warm each tortilla briefly in the skillet and fill with meat mixture and salsa as desired.

Tinfoil Bistro

For twists on the classic foil dinner, try the following combinations. Combine all ingredients and wrap in foil using the butcher's wrap method (see page 27). Cook on the coals for 10 minutes per side. Each recipe serves 1.

Asian Chicken

1 boneless, skinless
  chicken breast

$^1/_4$ cup teriyaki sauce
$^1/_4$ cup orange juice

2 cups frozen stir-
  fry vegetables

Swedish Bake

6–7 frozen Swedish
  meatballs, thawed
$^1/_4$ cup beef
  consommé soup
$^1/_2$ cup sour cream

2 red or new
  potatoes, diced
Dash ground black
  pepper

Dash allspice
Dash nutmeg

Seafood Steamer

3–4 fresh Manila
  clams, scrubbed
3–4 fresh mussels,
  scrubbed
3 large uncooked
  shrimp, peeled
  and deveined

1 firm fish fillet
  such as halibut or
  mahi mahi cut into
  2-inch chunks
2 red or new
  potatoes, diced
$^1/_2$ cup chicken broth

4 tablespoons
  melted butter
1 teaspoon minced
  garlic

Irish Roast

1 thick slice of
  cooked or canned
  corned beef

$^1/_4$ head cabbage
2 red potatoes, diced

Ground black pepper

Cowboy BBQ

3 thin slices uncooked
  beef brisket or
  flank steak

1/4 cup mesquite
  barbecue sauce
1 small onion sliced

1 baking potato,
  sliced with skin on

Marinara Meatballs

6-7 frozen Italian
  meatballs, thawed
1 cup bottled
  marinara sauce

1/4 cup grated
  Parmesan cheese

1 cup fresh ravioli
  or tortellini

Vanilla Rice Pudding

Serves 4–6

2 cups water
2 cups instant rice
2 (12-ounce) cans
  evaporated milk
$1/2$ teaspoon salt
$1/4$ cup butter

$3/4$ cup sugar
1 teaspoon vanilla
  extract
1 teaspoon nutmeg
3 eggs, beaten

Equipment

Camp stove
Heavy saucepan

1. Bring water to a boil in a heavy saucepan. Slowly add rice. Cover and simmer 8–10 minutes until rice is soft.

2. Add milk, salt and butter to the rice, and bring to a boil. Reduce heat and simmer 5 minutes. Add sugar, vanilla and nutmeg to the beaten eggs. Slowly pour the egg mixture into the rice, stirring constantly until rice is thickened. Allow to cool slightly and serve for breakfast or dessert.

Trout Florentine

Serves 2

2 trout, cleaned
and dressed
1/2 cup dry breadcrumbs
2 tablespoons
butter, melted
2 cups fresh baby
spinach leaves,
chopped

1 teaspoon diced
garlic
3 green onions,
thinly sliced
1/2 cup chicken
broth or stock
1 teaspoon lemon juice
Salt
Ground black pepper

Equipment

Campfire coals
Heavy-duty
aluminum foil

1. Place each trout on a sheet of aluminum foil, shiny side facing up. Mix the
    breadcrumbs with the melted butter and stuff each trout. Continue stuffing with
    spinach, garlic and green onions. Drizzle stuffing with chicken broth and lemon
    juice. Add a dash of salt and black pepper. Wrap in foil and cook over the coals
    6 minutes per side.

2. Alternately, sauté each stuffed trout in a skillet over medium heat in 1 cup
    chicken stock and 2 teaspoons garlic.

# Green Apple and Cranberry Salad

Serves 2-4

$^1/_4$ cup mayonnaise
2 tablespoons
   lemon juice

$^1/_2$ teaspoon salt
2 crisp green apples,
   cored and chopped

$^1/_2$ cup candied walnuts
1 cup dried
   cranberries

In a mixing bowl, whisk together mayonnaise and lemon juice. Add remaining ingredients and stir gently to coat.

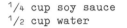 # Teriyaki Beef

Serves 2-4

1/4 cup soy sauce
1/2 cup water

1 teaspoon ground
  ginger
1/2 teaspoon
  garlic powder

1/4 cup brown sugar
1 pound flat-iron
  or flank steak

1. Combine all ingredients in a large gallon-size Ziploc freezer bag and marinate for at least 4 hours or preferably overnight.

2. On a hot grill over a fire or charcoal, grill steak 6–8 minutes per side until slightly charred on the outside. Slice and serve with vegetables and rice.

Japanese-Style Vegetables

Serves 2–4

1 (12-ounce) bag
  shelled frozen
  edamame
2 cups baby carrots
1 small onion, chopped
$1/4$ cup rice wine
  vinegar

$1/4$ cup water
$1/2$ teaspoon salt

Equipment

Charcoal briquettes,
  campfire coals or
  cook on camp stove
12-inch Dutch oven,
  10 coals on bottom,
  16 coals on top,
  350 degrees F

Place ingredients in a Dutch oven and cook with heat on top and bottom for
20 minutes.

Berry Pie

Serves 8

Pie Crust

4 cups flour
2 teaspoons salt

$^1/_4$ cup butter
1 cup shortening

$^1/_4$–$^1/_3$ cup water

Filling

4 tablespoons all-
  purpose flour
1$^1/_4$ cup sugar
1 teaspoon almond
  extract
1 teaspoon vanilla
  extract
2 teaspoons
  lemon juice

1 (16-ounce) package
  frozen or fresh
  raspberries, thawed
1 (16-ounce)
  package frozen
  or fresh sliced
  strawberries, thawed
4 tablespoons
  butter, melted
1 egg, beaten
Coarse sugar

Equipment

Charcoal briquettes
  or campfire coals
12-inch Dutch oven,
  10 coals on bottom,
  16 coals on top,
  350 degrees F

1. Using a fork, cut the dry pie crust ingredients into the butter and shortening until crumbly. Add water a little at a time, until dough forms. Try to not overwork the dough. Cover with plastic wrap and chill.

2. For the filling, mix flour and sugar together in a bowl. Add extracts and lemon juice and gently fold in berries.

3. Separate dough into 2 balls and roll out both crusts to $^1/_4$ inch thick. Place 1 crust in the bottom of the Dutch oven, pulling it at least halfway up the side. Add berry mixture and cover with the remaining pie crust or cut into strips to form a lattice top. Pinch edges between thumb and forefinger to scallop. Add the melted butter to the beaten egg and brush the top with the mixture. Sprinkle with coarse sugar.

4. Cover and bake with heat on top and bottom for about 30 minutes until crust is brown and pie is bubbly.

Icebox Ice Cream

Serves 2–4

1¹/₂ cups cream
¹/₂ cup milk
¹/₂ cup sugar
3 tablespoons instant
  vanilla pudding

¹/₂ teaspoon vanilla
Fruit, nuts, candy
  bars, cookies or
  other mix-ins
  as desired

Equipment

Large mixing bowl
  filled with ice
1-quart jar or water
  bottle with lid
1 box rock or
  kosher salt

1. Combine all ingredients and pour into the 1-quart container.

2. Sprinkle salt in layers throughout the ice in the large mixing bowl. Place container with ingredients in the center of the ice, covering well. Take turns spinning and turning the container. About every 5 minutes, remove the lid and scrape frozen ice cream off the sides. In about 30–40 minutes, the ice cream should be ready to serve. The longer it's left in ice, the firmer the ice cream will be.

Gourmet Three-Day Menu

Day 1
Dinner: Tinfoil
    Bistro—Marinara
    Meatballs,
    Tinfoil Garlic
    Bread, Berry Pie

Day 2
Breakfast: Sausage
    and Pepper
Breakfast
    Burritos,
    Fresh Fruit
Lunch: Cranberry
    Walnut Salad
    with Crusty
    French Bread
Dinner: Manicotti,
    Mixed Greens,
    Shepherd Cheese
    Bread with
Roasted Garlic
    Spread, Icebox
    Ice Cream

Day 3
Breakfast:
    Sourdough
    Pancakes, Vanilla
    Rice Pudding

The Spice Rack

To really unleash your creativity as a camp cook, you'll need to bring along a portable spice rack. Often dollar or discount stores will carry extra-small-sized spices in jars, which are great for occasional camp cooking. A basic spice rack should include ground black pepper, garlic powder, dried parsley, Italian seasoning, sage, thyme, nutmeg, cinnamon, chili powder, lemon pepper and cayenne pepper. Make a note of which spices you use frequently at home and add them to your collection. A small tool or tackle box with a deep gear tray makes a great portable spice rack that is easy to use.

Fresh herbs and spices add special flavor and are often overlooked. When filling the ice chest, don't forget to add fresh cilantro, basil and Italian parsley. Fresh rosemary Is particularly useful to impart an outdoor flavor to foods.

Open-Fire Grilling

Many campgrounds have fires with metal grates for cooking. Outdoor stores also sell portable fire grates. While it takes practice creating a good bed of coals for grilling over an open fire, cooking on a grate is a great way to add flavor to meats. Keep in mind that hardwoods impart the best flavor while many soft woods may have off-taste smoke due to high sap contents if the wood isn't properly seasoned. One alternative is to bring along a bag of mesquite or hickory hardwood chips to sprinkle on a low bed of coals.

Matching Foods to the Scenery

Camping is a great way to experience the beauty of nature. Planning menus with dishes to enhance the experience can be a lot of fun. Think about the environment in which you'll be as well as the weather. The American southwest lends itself perfectly to foods inspired by the flavors of Mexico, while camping in colder temperate forests may call for warm and earthy comfort foods. If fishing is a part of your vacation plans or you'll be camping in coastal areas, plan to cook fresh dishes with local ingredients. Often on the way to your campsite you'll pass through small towns. Check out the local markets for seasonal specialties that can be incorporated into your meals.

Backpacking

If camping is getting back to nature, backpacking takes it up a notch, really allowing a person to become more of a part of nature. You're on the trail, often miles away from reminders of modern life, reliant on what you can carry for shelter and food. Cooking well for groups while backpacking presents unique challenges. Look to the following recipes for ideas and inspiration.

Hiker's Cereal

Serves 1–2

2 cups granola

$1/3$ cup instant dry
milk powder

$1/2$ cup Craisins
$1/4$ cup brown sugar

Pack all ingredients in a quart-size Ziploc freezer bag. When ready to prepare, add 1 cup cold water and shake. Eat out of bag with a spoon.

GORP

Makes 11 cups

4 cups Cheerios	2 cups salted peanuts	1 cup chocolate chips
2 cups raisins	2 cups M&M candies	

Combine all ingredients in a large mixing bowl. Separate into individual Ziploc sandwich bags.

★★★

Breakfast Wraps

Serves 1

1 cup dehydrated hash browns	2 flour tortillas	2 strips precooked bacon
1 cup boiling water	1/4 cup shredded cheddar cheese or cheese powder	1 small packet ketchup
		Salt
		Ground black pepper

Rehydrate the hash browns by adding boiling water. Wait 15 minutes until hydrated, and divide evenly on tortillas. Top with cheese, bacon and ketchup. Season to taste. Wrap and eat.

Pita Sandwiches

Serves 1

1 (2.4-ounce) hummus
  single pack
1 pita flatbread

Sun-dried tomatoes
  as desired
1 (4-ounce) can
  sliced olives

$^1/_2$ cup shredded
  Parmesan cheese

Spread hummus on pita flatbread and sprinkle with tomatoes, olives and cheese.

★★★

Avocado Bacon Wrap

Serves 1-2

1 single-serve
  packet mayonnaise
2 flour tortillas

1 ripe avocado, sliced
2 slices precooked
  bacon

Salt to taste

Spread mayonnaise evenly over each tortilla and top with avocado and bacon. Add salt and roll up.

Sweet Mix

Serves 4-6

1 cup corn syrup
1/4 cup butter, melted

8 cups Rice Chex
   cereal

1/2 cup slivered
   almonds

Mix corn syrup and melted butter and heat in a microwave on high for about
1 1/2 minutes. Pour over Rice Chex cereal. Add almonds. Spread on a cookie sheet
and bake at 300 degrees for 8–10 minutes, stirring midway through baking. Allow
to cool. Package in individual Ziploc sandwich bags.

★★★

Pizza Bagels

Serves 1

1 (8-ounce) can
   tomato sauce

1 bagel, sliced
1 tablespoon Italian
   seasoning

1/4 cup Parmesan
   cheese, shredded

Spread tomato sauce on both sides of the bagel. Sprinkle with Italian seasoning and
cheese. Toast in a skillet over a stove or wrap in foil and place on campfire coals for
5–8 minutes.

Tomato Noodles

Serves 1

1 cup dry egg noodles
1 package tomato
  Cup-a-Soup mix
2 cups water
1/4 teaspoon Italian
  seasoning

1/4 cup textured
  vegetable protein,
  beef flavor
  (optional)

Equipment

Backpacking stove
Small saucepan

Combine all ingredients in a saucepan and bring to a boil. Reduce heat and simmer 10 minutes until cooked.

★★★

Spicy Asian Noodles

Serves 1

1 package ramen
  noodles, any flavor
2 cups water
1/2 cup dried shiitake
  mushrooms
1/2 cup dried corn

2-3 cured and dried
  teriyaki beef
  strips (optional)
1 single-serve
  packet soy sauce
Hot pepper sauce
  to taste

Equipment

Backpacking stove
Small saucepan

Combine all ingredients except soy and hot pepper sauce and boil for 3–6 minutes. Season to taste.

Masala Chicken and Rice

Serves 1-2

1 cup instant
  white rice
2 cups water
1 package Cream
  of Chicken Cup-
  a-Soup mix

$^1/_2$ teaspoon paprika
$^1/_2$ teaspoon
  ground cumin
$^1/_2$ teaspoon cinnamon
1 (5-ounce) can
  chicken (optional)

Equipment

Backpacking stove
Small saucepan

Combine all ingredients in a saucepan. Bring to a boil, turn down to simmer and cover until rice is tender and sauce is thickened.

★★★

Split Pea Soup

Serves 1-2

4 cups water
2 cups dried peas
2 cubes beef bouillon

4 strips precooked
  bacon, cut
  into pieces

Equipment

Backpacking stove
Small saucepan

At breakfast, bring water to a boil and add peas. Turn off heat and cover. Let sit 6–8 hours until peas are soft and then return to heat. Add bouillon cubes and bacon pieces and cook for 10 minutes.

Caramel Cheesecake Dessert

Serves 2–4

1 small box instant
  cheesecake flavor
  pudding (substitute
  white chocolate
  or vanilla)

1 cup dry powdered
  milk
1 caramel candy
  bar, chopped (Rolo
  or Caramello)

3 graham crackers,
  chopped
2 cups cold water

Combine all ingredients except water in a gallon-size Ziploc freezer bag. When ready to prepare, add water to the bag and shake and knead to mix. Allow to stand for at least 5 minutes in a cool place before serving.

Three-Day Backpack Menu

Day 1
Lunch: Avocado
  Bacon Wrap, Gorp
Dinner: Masala
  Chicken and Rice,
  Fresh Fruit

Day 2
Breakfast:
  Breakfast Wraps,
  Sweet Mix
Lunch: Pita
  Sandwiches
Dinner: Split Pea
  Soup, Cheesy
  Bread, Caramel
  Cheesecake
  Dessert

Day 3
Breakfast:
  Hiker's Cereal
Lunch: Pizza
  Bagels
Dinner: Tomato
  Noodles, Parmesan
  and Olive Oil
  Couscous

Groups and Backpacking

Backpacking in a group presents special challenges. The more people in a group, the greater the stress on the environment when setting up camp. It's more difficult to purify enough water and take care of sanitation needs, and cooking with lightweight backpacking stoves for more than 2 or 3 people is also a challenge. Ideally, a backpacking group should be made up of 6 or fewer people. Plan on having 1 stove per 2 people. While cooking systems do exist for up to 4 people, you are often limited to just boiling water for rehydrating freeze-dried meals. It's important to allow for 1 water-purification system per 2 people. Usually 1 person carries the stove and the other carries the water-purification system.

Grocery Store Meals

While freeze-dried backpacking meals are definitely lightweight and relatively easy to prepare, they do have drawbacks. They can be expensive and also tend to be over seasoned, especially when eaten at altitude or on extended trips. By creating menus from ingredients found at the grocery store, you can save money and tailor your meal to your tastes. Ingredients can be packaged in Ziploc bags and prepared in advance just like commercial freeze-dried food.

Cooking Systems

Backpacking and mountaineering cooking systems have advanced tremendously in the last decade. While liquid-fuel-based and gas-canister-based systems are still the 2 dominant types of stoves, integrated systems that feature cooking vessels engineered to be mated to a dedicated stove for increased efficiency have arrived on the market. What type of stove you buy is best determined by your cooking style. The integrated systems such as the Jetboil and the MSR Reactor are very lightweight and are primarily designed to boil water quickly. This is also important when melting snow. The older-style backpacking stoves are less efficient at boiling water and are heavier, but they are generally more versatile for other types of cooking including sautéing and frying.

Altitude Considerations

While an often-quoted research study on airline food suggested that taste buds are dulled by exposure to altitude, my experience as well as anecdotal evidence suggests this to be opposite from the fact. When on extended backpacking trips above 8,000 feet, I've found those in my group tend to be more sensitive to spicy flavors. Whether this is due to the drier air or less oxygen, I'm not sure.

Water boils at a lower temperature for every foot above sea level you travel, meaning foods cook slower. At extreme altitudes, foods such as pasta may not cook at all. Take this into consideration when planning for fuel requirements.

Index

Zac Williams

has been camping, cooking and taking photos since he was a scout.
He is the author of several cookbooks including *French Fries,
Little Monsters Cookbook, Little Aliens Cookbook,* and, his newest,
Little Cowpokes Cookbook. Zac lives in Pleasant View, Utah,
with his wife and three children.

Check out these other outdoor cookbooks at gibbs-smith.com